The Influence of a Father
The Study Guide

How You Can Be The Role Model and Mentor Your Children Need

The Influence of a Father
The Study Guide

Gateway Create Publishing
500 South Nolen #300
Southlake, TX 76092

ISBN: 978-0-9895167-9-2

Printed in the United States of America

tomlanebooks.com
gatewaycreate.com

How to Use the Curriculum

This curriculum is designed around the idea that group members will read *The Influence of a Father* by Tom Lane on their own time, before the group meeting.

Each week contains the following components:

1. **READ**

   Each group member will be reading the chapters on their own each week.

2. **WEEKLY INTRODUCTION**

   Read the introductory content for that week's study.

3. **CONNECT**

   Talk through the icebreaker questions to get people talking, engaged and comfortable with each other.

4. **DISCUSS**

   Discuss the questions.

5. **PRAY/HEAR**

   Because prophecy hinges on hearing God, allow time not only for prayer but also for group members to hear God speak.

6. **DIG DEEPER**

   Take some time individually after the meeting to process through what was discussed and what God spoke.

7. **REMEMBER**

   This is a list of key points or takeaways from the week's message.

Keys to a Dynamic Small Group

RELATIONSHIPS

Meaningful, encouraging relationships are the foundation of a dynamic small group. Teaching, discussion, worship and prayer are important elements of a group meeting, but the depth of each element is often dependent upon the depth of the relationships between the members.

AVAILABILITY

Building a sense of community within your group requires members to prioritize their relationships with one another. This means being available to listen, care for one another and meet each other's needs.

MUTUAL RESPECT

Mutual respect is shown when members value others' opinions (even when they disagree) and are careful to never belittle or embarrass others in the group.

OPENNESS

A healthy small group environment encourages sincerity and transparency. Members treat each other with grace in areas of weakness, allowing each other room to grow.

CONFIDENTIALITY

To develop authenticity and a sense of safety within the group, each member must be able to trust that things discussed within the group will not be shared outside of the group.

SHARED RESPONSIBILITY

Group members will share the responsibility of group meetings by using their God-given abilities to serve at each gathering. Some may greet, some may host, some may teach, etc. Ideally, each person should be available to care for one another as needed.

SENSITIVITY

Dynamic small groups are born when the leader consistently seeks and is responsive to the guidance of the Holy Spirit, following His leading throughout the meeting as opposed to sticking to the "agenda." This is especially important during the discussion and ministry time.

FUN!

Dynamic small groups take the time to have fun! Create an atmosphere for fun, and be willing to laugh at yourselves every now and then!

1

NEVER UNDERESTIMATE YOUR INFLUENCE AS A FATHER.

WEEK ONE

The Heritage of a Father

READ

Be sure you have completed reading the Introduction and Chapter 1 of *The Influence of a Father* before this week's meeting.

WEEKLY INTRODUCTION

Read the section below before moving on to the CONNECT section.

Hello, and welcome to our group. We're so glad you've decided to join us on this journey to discover *The Influence of a Father*. During the next few weeks, we'll be studying the topic of fathers and fathering. Whether you have a father, you are a father or you want to be a father; whether your children are two or twenty, there is so much to be learned from our heavenly Father on this subject!

Maybe you're thinking, "I didn't have a good relationship with my dad; I don't know how to parent my children!" Or you might even be saying to yourself, "I had a *great* dad! I know all about this fathering thing!" Maybe your children are grown, and you're convinced there's nothing left to do. Great news! God, our perfect Father, has things to say to you—to all of us!

Throughout this study, we will search together the Father's heart for His children. In doing so, we'll discover His principles that we as earthly fathers can follow as we strive to help our children grow into the godly men and women they were created to be.

Never underestimate your influence as a father. According to one study, students' view of God was directly correlated to their experience with their own fathers. If their earthly dad was absent and uninvolved, they tended to see God that way too. If, however, Dad was present, active and involved, no matter how imperfect, they leaned toward seeing God as a loving Father who is intimately interested in their lives. You have *direct influence* over the spiritual lives of your children—whether they are infants or adults. This is laid out so clearly for us in Exodus.

> *"For I, the Lord your God, am a jealous God, visiting the iniquity of the fathers upon the children to the third and fourth generations of those who hate Me, but showing mercy to thousands, to those who love Me and keep My commandments."* (Exodus 20:5–6)

The ripple effect that you as a father can have on many, many future generations is inestimable. Your influence has the power to change your children's lives—for good or bad. Sobering, yes—but infinitely powerful as we partner with God and His vision for our children. He's the one who knit them together in the first place!

So whether you're at the beginning of your fathering journey or on what you might perceive as the end, take the time during our journey together to explore your own views of God as Father, your relationship with your earthly dad and your influence over your own children. Relax—He's got it!

CONNECT

If you have children, briefly describe one of your favorite "fathering" moments with them. How do you think those moments impacted your children? If you don't have children, briefly recall one of your favorite moments with your own father. How did those moments impact you?

DISCUSS

- List some of your goals as a father.

- According to the book, what is the principle of transference, as described on page 5?

- Read Psalm 139. According to this chapter, what kind of a father is God? List some of the characteristics.

- What characteristics does He seek to transfer to us as His children?

> *Birth is not an accident. His hand guides the biological process of conception so that each person is the product of God's will and work.* (*The Influence of a Father,* page 13)

Pause for a moment and consider your views on the topic of life and conception. Believe it or not, your opinions on this subject will directly affect your ability to transfer God's heart to your children.

> *"Before I formed you in the womb I knew you; before you were born I sanctified you; I ordained you a prophet to the nations."* (Jeremiah 1:5)

As a parent, it's crucial that the truth that God is the creator and owner of all things be settled in your heart. Your children are precious gifts, directly from God to you!

> *Without my father's influence, I might live as many men today, viewing God only in religious terms or not viewing Him at all, holding to the opinion that religion is for preachers, the elderly, women and children. Real men do not need God, goes the mindset.* (*The Influence of a Father,* page 15)

- How have the men in your life viewed God? Do they see following Him as a sign of weakness or strength? How have their views shaped yours?

> *We must have a personal relationship with God to be able to transfer it to our children.* (*The Influence of a Father,* page 17)

- Stop for a moment. In order to pass along these values to our children, we must have a relationship with God ourselves. Where are you in this process? Is God simply a religious concept? Or have you come to know Him personally? If you cannot say with certainty that you have a vibrant, living relationship with Him, re-read pages 16–18 in *The Influence of a Father*, taking time to pray and ask God where you stand with Him. Journal your experience here.

____

____

____

____

____

____

____

____

PRAY / HEAR

Let's pause here just for a minute. Talking about fathers and fathering may bring up some painful wounds from your past. Maybe your father wasn't a good father; maybe he was absent; maybe he was abusive. Whatever your experience with your earthly father, God wants to heal those hurt places and show you what a good, kind, loving and present Father He is.

First of all, you may need to admit to yourself that your father's choices hurt you. As men, we're often convinced that to admit pain is to admit weakness; but God can't heal what you won't share with Him. Take just a minute and ask Him:

- Lord, what hurts am I carrying as a result of my father's choices? (Pause a moment and listen for His answer. Journal what you hear.)

Now pray something like this:

- Lord, today I choose to forgive my father. I choose to release him of any responsibility or debt I may have felt he owed me.

DIG DEEPER

Read the following passages and journal the characteristics of God you find in each passage.

- John 6:45
- Acts 2:33
- Romans 1:7
- Romans 8:15
- Galatians 1:4
- Ephesians 1:17
- 1 Thessalonians 3:13
- Hebrews 12:7

- As you begin your journey through this study, ask God to show you who He is as a Father. Listen for His answers and journal them here.

____

____

____

____

____

____

REMEMBER

- Children are a gift from God. (See Psalm 127:3.)
- What we model and transfer to our children through our behavior must be a reflection of God and His plans for our life and theirs.
- We will **transfer** to our children the values and character demonstrated in our own lives.
- There are two foundational truths that should radically shape our view of our parenting role:
  - > God is the creator and owner of all things; and
  - > We are responsible to Him for our actions.
- We must have a personal relationship with God to be able to transfer it to our children.

*(**Note:** For those who would like additional resources or further ministry in this area, please see your group leader.)*

NEXT WEEK

Read chapters 2, 3 and 4 before next week's meeting.

NOTES

2

Our responsibility as fathers is to identify the foolishness and correct it by aiming them in the direction of connection with the Lord.

WEEK TWO

Establishing Standards for a Father's Influence

READ

Be sure you have completed reading chapters 2, 3 and 4 of *The Influence of a Father* before this week's meeting.

WEEKLY INTRODUCTION

Read the section below before moving on to the CONNECT section.

Welcome back! I hope you're enjoying our journey together. There really is no joy like that of being a parent!

Last week, we spent some time laying a foundation for the importance of a father's influence in the lives of his children. This week, we're going to dig more deeply into that influence, discussing some basic principles regarding children and what the Bible has to say about them. We'll take a closer look at some of the characteristics of God and how He relates to us as Father, and we'll continue our journey of learning how to transfer those characteristics to our children.

While the Bible clearly states in Psalm 127 that children are a gift from the Lord, it also tells us in Proverbs that there is foolishness in the heart of every one of those children. If you've ever been around a small child (or even an older one, for that matter) for more than about 10 minutes, you know this to be true. Our responsibility as fathers is to identify the foolishness and correct it by aiming them in the direction of connection with the Lord.

How do we do that? First of all, we need to know what foolishness looks like. Understanding the difference between "foolishness" and "childishness" is crucial. As parents, we walk a fine line between helping our child drive out what doesn't belong and punishing them for something they can't help. Secondly, as we model and grow in our own understanding of godliness, we transfer those precepts to our children and ask them to follow in our footsteps.

And thirdly, we must instill a healthy fear of the Lord. We must teach our children reverence for Him. Proverbs tells us that "the fear of the Lord is the beginning of wisdom." It is a primary goal of parenting to launch our children into the world as adults with wisdom, right? Therefore, we must begin with an understanding of what "the fear of the Lord" really means.

Setting these parameters in place allows us to have the influence on our children we are designed and commissioned by God to have. They provide the framework for instilling our values from a place of godliness and integrity.

Come on. Let's dig in.

CONNECT

- Describe a time from your childhood when your "foolishness" reared its ugly head. How did your father respond? How did you respond?

DISCUSS

Our children's potential is in our hands as it relates to taming the negative instincts and cultivating the positive virtues within them. This is the reality of positive parenting, and no father can succeed without understanding the capacity for foolishness common to all men. (*The Influence of a Father,* page 23)

Foolishness is bound up in the heart of a child. (Proverbs 22:15)

- What does "foolishness" mean? Define it in your own terms.

- As a father, what sort of behavior do you expect from your child? Many men respond to foolishness in their children with a combination of anger and impatience, as if the children should "know better." What, according to the book, might this cause in children (*The Influence of a Father,* page 24)?

- Read the rest of Proverbs 22:15. What does the Bible say will get rid of the foolishness in a child's heart?

- Who was the primary disciplinarian in your house when you were a child? Describe that experience.

- Who is the primary disciplinarian in your house now? Describe how you see your role in relation to your children's mother. What does the Bible say about the role of a father in the house?

- Read and discuss Ephesians 6:4. What does it mean to "provoke" someone? What instruction does the verse give regarding fathers?

- It's been said that "we don't know what we don't know." How might this principle apply to children?

- Earlier in this study, we introduced the idea of "transference," meaning that we transfer our values to our children through our parenting. Pause for a moment and consider this question: "What am I trying to transfer to my children?" Write your thoughts here.

  ____

  ____

  ____

  ____

- Read Deuteronomy 6:6–7. What parenting instructions does this verse give? Discuss ways in which you can begin to implement these things in your own house.

With kids, if you say it, you better mean it, and more importantly, you better be doing it. (*The Influence of a Father,* page 39)

- Discuss this statement. Is it true that "more is caught than taught"? What are some things you "caught" from your parents? What are some things your children might be "catching" from you?

- What thoughts come to mind when you hear or read the phrase "the fear of God"? What do you think Proverbs 1:7 means when it says that "the fear of the Lord is the beginning of knowledge"?

- What are some synonyms for "fear"? Could those words be applied to God too?

- When our children disobey us, what should they fear? Our anger? No; instead we need to instill such a deep atmosphere of respect and connection with them that they fear anything that would threaten that connection. With God, what exactly should we fear? If we have been made new in Christ, we need no longer fear God's wrath or punishment. Instead, we should fear disconnection from Him—from a close, loving relationship with the one who loves us best.

PRAY / HEAR

Take a moment and ask God a few questions. Give Him time to answer! Journal what you hear.

- "God, am I being a good example for my children? Has my character been consistent with the principles I am trying to teach them?" Is there any area in which I have allowed inconsistencies to creep in?

- "Fear" can be a difficult word for us to associate with God, especially if our earthly fathers used anger or intimidation in an attempt to control us.

- "Father, have I been *afraid* to come to You? In what ways did my father show me an inaccurate view of You? Today, I choose to forgive my father for those things. Would You show me the truth about You? Would You show me the truth of how You see me as a son?" (Don't forget to write down what you hear!)

- God, would You show me what "fun" looks like? (Don't forget to journal what you hear!)

DIG DEEPER

"*We can only transfer what we have*" (*The Influence of a Father,* page 35). In light of this truth, take a moment and examine whether or not you truly have the things you are trying to transfer to your children.

- Look for those "teaching moments" this week (opportunities to discuss godly principles with your children). Also, look for ways to show your children how fun God really is!

- Allow God to father you, too. Allow Him to use "teaching moments" in your life. Journal what He shows you!

____

____

____

____

____

____

REMEMBER

- A successful father is one who is able to correct foolish behavior without inflicting emotional hurt.
- We can only transfer what we have.
- Our children are influenced more by the life we model for them than by what we say, our good intentions or any other factor of influence.
- Our children's view of God is directly shaped by their interactions with us.
- Every day is full of "teaching moments" with our children.

- Do not link acceptance of your children with their performance. They must know that they are always accepted, regardless of their behavior.

NEXT WEEK

Be sure you read chapters 5–10 before next week's meeting. We are going to take two weeks to study these chapters.

NOTES

3

Men of integrity recognize that mistakes are inevitable, and they strive to take responsibility for their actions.

WEEK THREE

Transferring Standards through a Father's Influence, Part 1

READ

Be sure you have completed reading chapters 5 and 6 of *The Influence of a Father* before this week's meeting.

WEEKLY INTRODUCTION

Read the section below before moving on to the CONNECT section.

Hello, and welcome back. Over the past couple of weeks, we've begun to examine our fathering experiences—whether from our own father or as we have parented our own children. We've discussed the foundational idea of transference and how we as fathers pass down what we have within us. We've begun to lay some groundwork that will allow us to continue our lifelong goal of truly fathering our children from a godly and biblical perspective.

As adults, we understand the value of character. We understand the value of a good name and how we provide an example of who God is through our integrity—or lack thereof.

This week, we are going to focus on the word "character" and what it really means. We are going to explore some ways in which we can intentionally guide and shape our children's journey toward becoming men and women of character, accurately representing God to the world around them.

We know that integrity is important. We know we need it. But how do we get it? It doesn't just happen.

Galatians 5:22–23 are familiar verses to most of us; they lay out the "fruit" of the Spirit—those things that should be a visible result of our ongoing relationship with, and infilling of, the Holy Spirit. The list includes things like love, joy, peace, patience, kindness, goodness, faithfulness, gentleness and self-control. According to the Word of God, learning to control ourselves should be an outcome of our spiritual growth.

But how do we teach self-control? As we've previously discussed, we teach most of these principles intentionally—and by example. The first thing we need to do as fathers is to examine our own ability to manage ourselves. How do we handle situations that arise? Do we take responsibility for our own actions or do we cast blame on others? Are we in control of our emotional and spiritual health or are we easily angered? Easily swayed?

Men of character happen to the world around them, not the other way around. Men of integrity recognize that mistakes are inevitable, and they strive to take responsibility for their actions. Godly fathers walk in a spirit of self-control and teach their children to do the same. After all, the goal of parenting is to raise adults who can take care of themselves, right?

Ready? Here we go.

CONNECT

- Review the story on pages 79–80 in *The Influence of a Father*. Describe a similar experience from your own life. How did your parents handle it? How did you handle it?

DISCUSS

- Read Galatians 5:16–25. List the works of the flesh found in verses 19–21. What things stand out to you? Are there any you may struggle or have struggled with?

- Now list the fruit of the Spirit in verses 22–23. What do you notice?

  ____

  ____

  ____

  ____

- While the things listed are indeed "fruit" of the Holy Spirit, they are by no means accidental or passive. According to this passage, Paul is clearly stating that we *have a choice* in how these things happen in our lives—both good and bad. At the very end of the list of fruit in verses 22–23 is "self-control." What does this mean? How does it affect the other fruit listed?

- According to Galatians, we are able to remain in control of ourselves, no matter what anyone else does. No one can "make us" do anything. Has the fruit of "self-control" been evident in your life? How do you respond when you make a mistake? How about when others make mistakes? Are your responses characterized by the list in Galatians 5:22–23?

Adam and Eve were presented with a choice—one that had clearly defined consequences: *"But of the tree of the knowledge of good and evil you shall not eat, for in the day that you eat of it* ***you shall surely die****"* (Genesis 2:17, emphasis added). God put a choice, right there in the garden. And Adam and Eve were free to choose! Did God have an opinion on what they should choose? Of course. But if He had set out to create a people who were truly free, He had to allow them the reality of choice.

- Read Genesis 3. What did Adam and Eve freely choose? How did God handle it? What were the consequences of their choices?

We are created in the image of a God who is fully in control of Himself. Throughout the Old Testament, the people of Israel—His children—displayed characteristics that He likely wished they had not displayed. They disobeyed Him regularly, abandoning their commitment to a loving and good Father. *And He let them.* When the consequences of their actions had been visited upon them, He lovingly walked them through those consequences. He rarely rescued them altogether; instead, He allowed them to experience the result of their choice.

- Describe a time when you were allowed to fully experience the consequences of your actions. What did you learn from that experience?

> *Parents play a beneficial role when they work with their children to discover the lesson to be learned in a difficult situation rather than being their child's champion and defender against all perceived injustice.* (*The Influence of a Father,* page 77)

We live in a society where our children are often perceived as victims and we as their necessary rescuers. Sometimes this is true, as in the case of dangerous or abusive situations. Often, however, we rescue our children from taking responsibility for their own choices rather than allowing them to learn from their mistakes. We allow them to blame others for their mistakes and failures and even model this in our own lives. This will never teach our children to have character and integrity. It will not teach them self-control; quite the contrary, it will perpetuate an attitude of victimhood or entitlement that will follow them throughout their lives.

Our goal as parents should be to impart to our children, through our example and intentionally guiding them through the circumstances of their lives, the sense that they are capable of managing themselves.

- What example do your children see? Describe a time when you had a choice to exercise self-control. Did you? How did that look? Be vulnerable. If the experience was less than your best, take a moment and examine how you could have chosen differently.

Character and *integrity* are present when our words and our actions line up with one another. When we do the thing we say we will do, when we are responsible for ourselves and our actions, we can transfer these values to our children.

When Jesus was on the cross, He was still fully in control of Himself, despite His circumstances.

> *"For this reason the Father loves Me, because I lay down My life so that I may take it again.* ***No one has taken it from Me, but I lay it down on My own initiative.*** *I have authority to lay it down, and I have authority to take it up again."* (John 10:17–18, NASB, emphasis added)

> *Faith is confident trust in the character of God.* (*The Influence of a Father,* page 89)

How was Jesus able to remain fully in control of Himself, even as He was being crucified? He had *confident trust in the character of God*. He knew that no matter what His circumstances were, God would still be God, and He, Jesus, still had full access to God's kingdom. This means, of course, that He had full access (even while being nailed to a piece of wood) to love, joy, peace, patience, kindness, goodness, gentleness and self-control. We have that same access, no matter what our circumstances are—and so do our children.

- What we truly believe about God and our access to Him is revealed when we are "squeezed." Like a lemon, what is inside will come out. What comes out when you get "squeezed" by the circumstances of your life? Is it love, joy, peace, patience and the other fruits of the Spirit? Or is it something else?

- Describe a time when you were "squeezed." What came out?

As a father, it is your role to point your children to the character of God. You do that by example, but also by intentionally teaching them to exercise the fruit of self-control.

PRAY / HEAR

Let's take some time and ask God to speak to us about this issue of self-control, character and integrity.

- Read the list of the fruit of the Spirit. Which fruit do you want? The Bible says we have not because we ask not (James 4:2). Ask Him for it! He will give it to you!

- Take a minute and journal the conversation you just had with God.

"Lord, I confess that at times I have chosen to blame others for my mistakes. I confess that I have not always been willing to accept responsibility for my own actions. I am sorry! Would You forgive me? (Don't forget to give Him time to answer!) Lord, today I choose to be responsible for my own actions. I choose to exert self-control and manage my own choices and consequences. I choose today to be a man of integrity, a man of my word—just like You."

DIG DEEPER

Recognize that "self-control" does not translate to being "controlling." It simply means that you will be in control of you no matter what anyone else does. Sometimes as a parent, that can be difficult. Spend some time this week paying close attention to your responses to others. Are you in control of you? Is the fruit of the Spirit evident in your life, no matter what your circumstances are?

- Take a few moments this week and journal your thoughts on this subject. ______________________________

____

____

____

____

____

____

REMEMBER

- Self-control is a fruit of the Spirit.
- Integrity and character are a result of self-control.
- *Character* and *integrity* are present when our words and our actions line up.
- As a father, it is your role to point your children to the character of God.

NEXT WEEK

Be sure to read chapters 7–10 before next week's meeting.

4

God is a kind and gracious Father who disciplines us out of love; any other method is not of Him.

WEEK FOUR

Transferring Standards through a Father's Influence, Part 2

READ

Be sure you have completed reading chapters 7–10 before this week's meeting.

WEEKLY INTRODUCTION

Read the section below before moving on to the CONNECT section.

Welcome back! We're about halfway through our study together. Last week, we continued our time together with a discussion of character: what is it, and how do we partner with God to build it in our children?

This week, we are going to tackle the big one. This week, we're talking about discipline.

This word can be a scary word for many people. The word "discipline" can bring up painful memories of misuse of disciplinary methods or even memories of abuse. Let me just stop, pause right here and say that I am so sorry if that was your experience. I am sorry that someone saw fit to use the idea of "discipline" to harm you in any way. This is not at all what God intended when He designed parents and children.

Discipline, according to God's methods, is not punishment. It is not revenge or control; in fact, true godly discipline is meant for the exact opposite. It is meant to provide guidance and accountability, bringing us and our children back onto the right path.

God's discipline is always redemptive. It is always out of love, and it is always meant to restore connection. "Sin" is anything that breaks our connection with God; discipline is meant to reconnect us with our heavenly Father, who loves us perfectly—no matter what we do. His methods of discipline always reflect His love for us. As parents, we are responsible to reflect the nature and character of God to our children—even when they mess up.

Many times, parents discipline out of wrong motives. They discipline out of anger, frustration, embarrassment, pride or inconvenience, and end up harming their children rather than helping them.

This week, we're going to discuss discipline. We'll examine how God disciplines us as His children, and discover how we as parents can more effectively communicate His nature and character to our children through correction. We'll discuss terms such as "submission" and "accountability" and how they relate to us as sons and daughters of God, and how they relate to our children.

If you have been wounded by wrong discipline, please know there is healing for you. At the end of our time today, your leaders will assist you in processing how to best seek healing for those hurt places in your life. God is a kind and gracious Father who disciplines us out of love; any other method is not of Him.

Lean in today. Allow Him to speak to you regarding your own relationship with Him, and that of your children. He loves you—and them—infinitely!

CONNECT

- What disciplinary methods were used in your house growing up? Were they effective or not? Why or why not?

DISCUSS

- Define "submission." Give examples from your own life. Consider things like traffic laws, TSA guidelines, your boss at work, etc. How does submission look in those cases?

- Submission must be chosen or it becomes slavery. We choose who and what we submit to. It is always easier to submit to a safe authority, one that has your best interest at heart. What kind of authority are you asking your children to submit to?

God provides us with an example of what authority looks like. His authority is kind, loving and gracious, never angry, arrogant, impatient or harsh. Submission to His authority is safe because I am convinced of His interest in my well-being. I am confident in His ability to care for me and to know what is best because of the connection we have.

- Children respond to connection too. They will more readily submit to an authority in which they feel safe. What can you do as a father to show your children they are safe with you?

  God's motive for correction is love; His reason is always redemptive. (*The Influence of a Father,* page 114)

- The purpose of correction is to maintain and/or restore connection. How is this different than you might have previously looked at correction and discipline?

- What are some other motivations for discipline (*The Influence of a Father,* page 114)? What are some possible effects of approaching discipline in this manner?

God doesn't use our failures to condemn and reject us, so we do not want to do that to our children. (*The Influence of a Father,* page 119)

The reality is your children will need discipline. As we discussed in Week 2 of our study, foolishness is bound up in the heart of our children, and they need our guidance and correction. But we must never shame our children as we administer discipline. God will never shame us for our mistakes, nor should we use shame as a method of correction.

- What does God require of us when we sin? Read 1 John 1:9. What is our part? What is God's?

Whichever method of discipline we choose, it must always be from a heart of love, compassion and restoration. We must strive to restore or maintain connection.

- Read Psalm 103:12. What does God say about what He does with our sin? In light of this verse, how should we handle our children's mistakes, once they have repented and received forgiveness?

- Define "accountability." List some characteristics necessary for true accountability. ________________________________

- Why might we need accountability in our lives?

- Describe some characteristics of a good mentor. Compare these characteristics to those of a good father.

- List any mentors you have had in your life. Do you have one now? Describe that relationship and the benefits of accountability in your life. ________________________________

- What are some reasons men might resist the accountability that mentoring provides? List any you recognize within yourself. What can you do to consciously choose to overcome this resistance?

You cannot mentor your children in accountable relationships until you have first made yourself accountable. (*The Influence of a Father,* page 131)

- You can only transfer what you have, and remember that more is often "caught than taught." How can you model accountability in your relationships?

God promises to use the circumstances of our lives to accomplish His good work. (*The Influence of a Father,* page 142)

- Read Romans 8:28. What does Paul mean by the phrase "all things"? What about the phrase "work together"?

- Think about a lesson you learned through circumstances. What happened? What did you learn as a result?

Parents must learn when to lend assistance to their children, when to come to their defense, how to support them, yet allow them to stand up and fight for themselves. (*The Influence of a Father,* page 153)

- Consider your children right now. How old are they? What are their capabilities? Weaknesses? Needs? Take a few moments and talk with God about how best to use the circumstances of their lives to teach them, allowing them to receive every instructional benefit of each situation.

- Review the three extreme parental responses listed on pages 146–152. Do you recognize any of your parents' parenting patterns? What about yours?

PRAY/HEAR

When a parent has disciplined out of a wrong heart, it can often lead to what we call *judgments* and *inner vows*. A judgment is a negative statement against something: "My father is angry and yells at me. Therefore, all men are angry." An inner vow is a response to a judgment we've made: "Because all men are angry, I will never trust a man again." In the case of a harsh or abusive father, it can lead to judgments and inner vows that will keep us from being able to parent our children in a healthy way. It can lead to abusive and controlling parenting; or, on the other end of the scale, passivity resulting from an unwillingness to reenact what was modeled for us.

Neither of these is healthy, so we need to deal with the judgments and inner vows we may have made. Let's take some time to talk to God about these things.

- *"Lord, what judgments have I made against You?" "Against others?"* Journal what you hear. ______________________

- *"Lord, what inner vows have I made as a result of these judgments?"* Journal what you hear. ______________________

- Confess: *"Yes, Lord. You're right. I did make these judgments and inner vows in my heart. I am sorry! Will You forgive me?"* (Wait for Him to answer you. He will!)

- *"Lord, what is the truth about these things?"* Journal what you hear.

  ____
  ____
  ____

- With your will, you made these judgments and inner vows. Now, with your will, choose to agree with the truth as He shows it to you. Journal your thoughts and feelings.

  ____
  ____
  ____

DIG DEEPER

- Describe your ideal relationship with your children. Consider the things we've discussed thus far in our study. What choices can you make this week to create an environment where that relationship is possible? ____

  ____
  ____

- In this process, you may discover you need to repent to your children for some things. Take some time and discuss those things with the Lord. Journal what you hear.

  ____
  ____
  ____

If you discover some areas of repentance, take them first to God. Re-read 1 John 1:9, and follow through. Then be open and honest with your children. Ask for their forgiveness.

Remember, though, that just like your relationship with your father, your children may have some wounds from your previous methods. Give them time to process those things with God.

If you don't currently have a mentor in your life, pray about whom to ask. God will show you. Then take the initiative and ask that person to consider it. Purpose in your heart to be fully accountable—to be submitted, teachable and correctable.

REMEMBER

- Submission is necessary for healthy relationships.
- Discipline must always come from a heart of love, compassion and restoration.
- Our highest goal must remain to have a connection with our children.
- True accountability is necessary for growth.
- God causes all things to work together for the good of those who love Him!

NEXT WEEK

Be sure to read chapters 11–15 before next week's meeting.

NOTES

5

YOU, AS A FATHER,

HAVE DIRECT INFLUENCE

OVER THE OUTCOME IN

YOUR OWN CHILD'S LIFE.

WEEK FIVE

Supporting Standards for a Father's Influence

READ

Be sure you have completed reading chapters 11–15 before this week's meeting.

WEEKLY INTRODUCTION

Read the section below before moving on to the CONNECT section.

Welcome back! We're in the home stretch of our time together.

I hope you've been encouraged by what you've heard and studied so far. Fatherhood is truly a great calling, one with far-reaching blessings for generations to come. It is not to be taken lightly, but can and should be a source of great joy and satisfaction in our lives.

Today, we're going to tackle a couple of different subjects. First, we're going to look at some practical steps we can take to maximize our influence as a father—such as spending time with your children, partnering with your wife and helping your children to discover their unique destiny.

It's difficult to have any relationship without spending time together. When you have a close friend, you want to spend time with that person! You want to talk, to listen, to be a part of their life and to enjoy things together. This is crucial for real intimacy to happen—to see and be seen by someone. However, many fathers don't view their children with this same perspective. Many men seem to be under the impression that children will grow themselves up or their wives will handle things, and they really don't need much from them—except maybe their wallets!

Does that sound ridiculous to you? It should, but yet statistics show that men are less likely to daily engage with their children than their wives, that there are many men who spend just a few minutes a day interacting with their children. If this is the case, who is fathering them? Who is calling out the greatness in your children? Who is identifying, supporting and guiding the unique destiny inherent in each of your children?

We'll examine the absolute necessity of your direct, daily, personal involvement with your children and how your partnership with your wife lays the foundation for your family as a whole. We'll discuss ways to identify and draw out the God-given destiny within your children and how to lead them into the fullness of that destiny.

Secondly, we'll spend some time discussing a unique and yet universal situation—teenagers. Parenting teens comes with its own set of challenges and rewards. It can be a time of great joy and victory or a time of discouragement and frustration. As young adults, our teens are walking a fine line between childhood and full adulthood, with physical, emotional and social changes happening at a rapid-fire pace. This time in a young person's life can be a time of growth and discovery with healthy boundaries and freedoms, or it can be a time of anger, pain and isolation. You, as a father, have direct influence over the outcome in your own child's life. I know that sounds daunting, but it should also be liberating! You can help! You, as a father, can be a catalyst for growth and health during a normally turbulent time.

Doesn't that sound hopeful? It should! No, it's not easy, but given time and attention, you'll come to find that you are raising some truly amazing people. What a privilege!

Ready to dig in? Here we go!

Have a great week!

CONNECT

- Describe your favorite memory from your teenage years.

DISCUSS

- Was your father present in your life? If he lived with you, did he spend time with you? Recount your favorite memory of your dad spending time with you. What happened? What did you talk about?

- Examine your schedule for the past week. How much time was built in to spend time with your children? If so, what did you do to interact directly with them? If not, what changes can you make in the near future?

- What is your favorite memory of spending time with your children? Describe where you were and what you did. How did they respond to you?

- Take a minute and brainstorm some things you can do to "make a memory" with your kids this week. Keep it simple: play a card game, take a walk and just let them talk, cook a meal together, read a book—the possibilities are endless. Take the time to enjoy them, no matter what age they are. Even infants crave eye contact with their parents! Let your child look at you. Let them see you!

- Jot down some ideas for spending time with your kids.

  ____

  ____

  ____

- Describe your parenting relationship with your spouse. How is she the same as you? How is she different?

- How do you view your differences? Do you see them as strengths that each of you bring to the table, or do you view them as things to be "fixed" so that she is more like you? *"Remember, if you're both the same, one of you is unnecessary!"* (*The Influence of a Father*, page 169)

- Define the word "destiny."

- Read Jeremiah 1:5 and Jeremiah 29:11. What do these scriptures tell us about how God sees us? What about His plans for us? Do you think He has these same plans for your children?

A father is to use his influence in [his children's] lives to help them discover their God-given destiny by developing and nurturing their strengths, desires, interests and abilities. (*The Influence of a Father,* page 178)

- Take a few moments and list your children's unique strengths and interests. List them individually.

____

____

____

- How are these things the same as yours? How are they different?

One of your (many) purposes in your child's life is to guide them to a place where they can fully walk in the destiny God has created for them. To do this, you must be connected to Him, walking in relationship so that you are in constant discussions with Him about them.

- You also must model this connection for your children. Remember, "more is caught than taught." How do they see your relationship with God? Do they see you in close talks with Him about your own destiny?

- What experiences can you provide for your child to help them discover their unique purpose? Discuss some options. Take some time to research. What are their passions? Interests? Hobbies? Talents?

- How do you handle failure in your life? How do you handle failure in the lives of your children? Do you see failure as an option? Why or why not?

Remember, God has created us all uniquely. Your children have fingerprints that no one else has! They also have destinies that no one else has. Allow them to display diversity—even if it's different than you—throughout their discovery process. Their path will be one God sets for them!

- How do you handle character flaws and attitude issues in your children? Go back to Weeks 3 and 4 and review the information there. These issues could keep your children from fully walking in their destinies! Guide them gently through God's growth process.

- What do you think of when you hear the word "teenagers"? How do you respond when you see them?

  The teenage years are an awkward stage of development between childhood and adulthood that present some interesting challenges to the parenting process. (*The Influence of a Father,* page 187)

- Describe yourself as a teenager. Be honest!

- It's crucial to remain connected to your teen. The principles we've discussed above still apply, but perhaps in some different ways. Discuss these differences. How does parenting change as your children approach young adulthood?

- What challenges may emerge during the teen years?

- The goal of parenting is to produce self-controlled adults. To do this, our teenagers must experience opportunities to control themselves—properly stewarding their freedom. What does this look like in your house?

- What can you do to continue to transfer your values to your teen, while allowing them to grow and mature?

PRAY / HEAR

Remember, we as fathers shape our children's image of God as Father. He is a kind, loving and *present* Father, always ready to listen, to talk, to be with us. Even one of His names—Emmanuel—means "God with us."

- Do you really believe that? Do you, in your heart, believe that God is interested in you? That He wants to be with you? We transfer our beliefs to our children; what beliefs about God are you transferring?

Let's clarify: a belief is not a thought. You can *think* that God is near and present and interested in your life, but if you *believe* otherwise, you won't pray, your Bible will seem dry and church will be an item on your checklist. Take just a moment and examine your own beliefs about God.

Ask Him these questions:

- *"God, what do I believe about You?"*

- *"God, would You show me right now just how close You are?"*

- *"God, do You want to spend time with me? How do You feel about me?"*

- He is waiting to spend time with You. He is the perfect Father, with all the time in the world for you. Don't forget to journal what you hear!

DIG DEEPER

- With your spouse, sit down this week and read Chapter 12 together. Take some time and discuss how you can better support each other in your parenting. Journal your thoughts!

- If you are divorced, and if it is possible, take a few minutes and discuss this topic with your ex-spouse. Resolve to put aside your own animosity and hurts as you seek to communicate with your children's mother. Your ultimate goal is a healthy partnership for the blessing and benefit of your children. Take a minute and write down your thoughts about this process.

- Take some time this week to examine your own influence. Are you stewarding it well, or are there some areas that may need some attention? Ask God to speak to you regarding those things. He has an opinion! Journal your thoughts.

REMEMBER

- It is crucial for fathers to spend time with their children.
- The mother of your children is your partner—and you hers—in parenting your children.
- God has created all of us with a unique destiny and purpose.
- Teenagers need Dad too!

NEXT WEEK

Be sure to read chapters 16–17 before next week's meeting.

6

Parenting never stops. Our children never "graduate" from their need for healthy interaction and guidance from us.

WEEK SIX

The Legacy Begins

READ

Be sure you have completed reading chapters 16–17 before this week's meeting.

WEEKLY INTRODUCTION

Read the section below before moving on to the CONNECT section.

Welcome to our final week together. I hope you have been challenged, encouraged and inspired by our time and you will step more fully into your crucial role as a father. If you're not one yet, I commend you for doing this work ahead of time. It will pay off—I promise!

But what if you're on the other end? What if you have grown children? What if those grown children have come back? We live in a society that has seen the emergence of what we call "boomerang" children—those who leave the nest but end up coming back. There are a variety of reasons for this—job loss, divorce, health issues, economic factors—just to name a few. For many parents, this has become a reality, and they are searching for answers. How do we parent an adult? Do they still need us? How involved—or uninvolved—should we be?

And what if their reasons for returning home involve problems and bad decisions? What then? Do we even let them back in to begin with? How much should we support them?

Parenting never stops. Our children never stop needing our strength and encouragement, no matter how old they are. But our role changes over time, as should our methods.

One role, however, that should never change no matter what our circumstances are, or that of our children, is our commitment to prayer. Our parenting is, simply put, nothing more than a partnership with God. It is, and should continue to be, a constant conversation with our heavenly Father who has their best interests in mind and sees the end from the beginning—even when we can't.

We cannot hope to succeed as parents without this relationship. Without prayer, we will inevitably lean on our own understanding—something the Bible cautions against. As a father, I need daily guidance and encouragement from my heavenly Father in order to be a good earthly dad. I can get those needs met by spending regular time in God's Word—and by spending time in His presence, talking and listening—by praying.

Perhaps you were raised to believe that you had to "do it all yourself." That to lean on anyone else, especially God, was a sign of weakness. This is quite common among men especially. But we as believers are designed to be daily plugged in to the One who made us, the One who knows our end from our beginning, the One who loves us perfectly. John 15 tells us to "abide"—to live in constant connection with our Source. This is never more evident than when we become fathers and we realize, perhaps for the first time, how much we need God in our lives, how much we need His strength and guidance as we take on the enormous responsibility of raising children.

Parenting never stops. Our children never "graduate" from their need for healthy interaction and guidance from us. Neither do we "graduate" from our need to depend on God. No matter what we do or how far we stray, He will always welcome us home.

Let's dig in for our final week. Ready? Here we go.

CONNECT

- Describe your current relationship with your own parents. Are you close? In what ways are they still involved in your life?

DISCUSS

- Begin by reading Luke 15:11–32. What was the father's response to the younger son's request in verse 12?

- Do you think the father in this story knew what his son was going to do with the money he received? Did he try to control his son's choices in any way?

  The resource the son received in the form of his inheritance was secondary to the support he received in the form of his father's permission to fail in his search. (*The Influence of a Father,* page 219)

- What was the son searching for? Why was it crucial for the father to allow him room to fail?

- Describe your own search for significance. Describe your own failures. How did your father respond?
- What is the biblical definition of "inheritance"? What, if any, conditions are attached to it? How does this definition compare to our modern concept of inheritance?
- How do you respond to your children's search for significance? How do you respond if and when they fail?
- Read Luke 15 (the entire chapter). How does the Father respond when we fail? How does He respond when we return?
- What is the difference between "empowering" and "enabling"? How might the story of the prodigal son have turned out if the father had enabled his son? What things might have been considered enabling instead of empowering?

Our first responsibility as parents is to help our children find their significance. (*The Influence of a Father,* page 217)

- Each child is unique in their design and calling. Our role as parents is not to control their choices, but rather to guide them to discover their own uniqueness in Him. Describe your children: what do you see that makes each of them unique?
- How have you empowered your children to discover their uniqueness?

- How have you responded when your children have made mistakes? How can you create a safe environment in which they can fail without fear of your response?

Despite the son's failure, the father at no time attempted to control his son or his son's choices. He never belittled, shamed or criticized him. Instead, he gave his son the freedom to fail, and then, when his son "came to his senses," freely received him without fear of rejection. If we are going to allow our children room to make mistakes and experience consequences, we must do so without controlling, manipulating, rejecting or shaming them.

- Read Luke 15:21–24 and 1 John 1:9. What is the Father's response when we, or our children, fail? What should our response to our children be?

  Parenting, at its core, is a partnership with God. (*The Influence of a Father,* page 227)

- According to page 228, what is the definition of *prayer*? How does this compare to your understanding of it?

- In your own life, how have you approached prayer in the past? Has it been relational and conversational or stale and perfunctory? Describe your previous prayer experience.

- Consider your own relationship with your children. As we've previously discussed, as fathers we should be approachable and safe. How do your children approach you?

- Why do we need to pray? Take a moment and examine your view of God's role. Do you see Him as "in control"—meaning He will do what He wants no matter what? Or do you view Him as a Father who is interested in the day-to-day details of His children? Describe how you see Him.

- We know that God is "sovereign." Many times, we assume that means He's a sort of cosmic puppet master, pulling the strings and doing what He likes. In fact, although God is absolutely in control of all of His creation, He has chosen to partner with us in fulfilling His plans on the earth and in fulfilling His plans for our children. He is intimately interested in our thoughts, feelings, opinions, frustrations, struggles, passions—He is intimately interested in us. He wants to know our hearts for our children: what do we hope for, long for, desire for them? He wants to know!

- Read Genesis 18:22–33. Describe Abraham's conversation with God. How did God respond to Abraham?

- Take a moment and examine your view of God in this light. Does God respond when we pray? How is this approach different than the way you might pray?

Finally, remember that *"God will uphold His end of the partnership!"* (*The Influence of a Father*, page 233) Trust Him to fulfill His promises. He loves your children more than you do!

PRAY/HEAR

- Take a moment and talk to God. Converse. Relate. Come close. Consider Abraham—do you think God wants to talk to you and relate to you the same way He did with Abraham?

Ask God this question:

- *"God, what would You like to talk about today?"* (Wait for Him to answer!) ______________________________
____
____
____

- Now, just take a few minutes and talk to your Father. He wants to hear what you have to say!

If you haven't already done so, consider starting a prayer journal. Use it to record your prayers for your children and God's responses to you. Don't forget to record answered prayer!

DIG DEEPER

- Take some time to examine your relationship with your grown children. Have you purposefully empowered them in their search for significance? Are there any ways in which you may have attempted to control or manipulate them? If and when they have failed, have you communicated rejection or shame in any way?

- Journal your thoughts here.

As we discussed in Week 4, one of our primary goals as parents is to maintain/restore connection with our children. If our responses to their failures have created disconnection, it is up to us to heal the breach and restore connection. Pray and ask the Lord what you may need to do to maintain relationship with your children.

- If your children are still at home, take some time to examine your current relationship with them. Are you empowering them at their current stage of exploration? What steps have you taken to ensure a safe place to fail and make mistakes?

- Most importantly, set aside time to pray. Invest in your partnership with God. Take some time to discuss your children, but also take some time just to be with Him. He longs for His children to be in His presence, just enjoying His company! Doesn't it delight you when your children just want to be with you? Imagine how your heavenly Father feels!

- Read Psalm 139 again. What does this chapter say about God's opinions and thoughts toward you?

During our study, we've examined our relationships with our own father, our children and our heavenly Father. These are all life-long relationships, and we can invest in them no matter how old they—or we—are. We can explore areas where we need to forgive, where we need forgiveness and where we can grow and change.

- Take a few moments and write down some highlights from our time together. How will your fathering be different from now on?

____

____

____

____

____

____

REMEMBER

- A father's primary responsibility is to reveal God to his children by teaching them about Him and His ways.
- We cannot project our dreams and goals onto our children. We must allow them to discover their own uniqueness in Christ.
- True significance can only be identified in connection with God.
- We should empower our children's search for purpose and significance without enabling them in an unhealthy way.
- Prayer is crucial to parenting! We must partner with God.
- God will uphold His end of the partnership—always.

NOTES

CPSIA information can be obtained at www.ICGtesting.com
Printed in the USA
BVOW10s2014160115

383733BV00004B/5/P

9 780989 516792